Art Museums
in the Vicinity of Moscow

Arkhangelskoye

A Country Estate
of the 18th and 19th
Centuries

Aurora Art Publishers
Leningrad

Compiled and introduced by
VALERY RAPOPORT

Designed by
VIACHESLAV ANDREYEV

Translated from the Russian by
PETER McCAREY

Photographs by
ALEXEI ALEXANDROV
and EDWARD STEINERT

Pavel Svinyin. 1788–1839. Country Estate of Arkhangelskoye. 1824. Watercolour. 22.5 × 36 cm

"The Russians have a feeling for the beauty of nature, and they know instinctively how to enhance it. Take, for example, the village of Arkhangelskoye, twelve miles from Moscow …," thus wrote the eminent Russian historian Nikolai Karamzin in his Notes on Sights in and around Moscow *(1817). And today, after a century and a half, Arkhangelskoye is still one of the most famous architectural complexes in the vicinity of Moscow.*

2 The Palace *(pls. 2–10)*
Entrance arch of the main courtyard. 1817
Designed by Stepan Melnikov
The gates
France (?). 1800–25
Cast iron and gilded bronze

3 A view, through the entrance arch, of the main
courtyard and the portico of the north façade

4 North façade. 1790s–1820s
Designed by Charles de Guerne

5   The main courtyard with the sculptural group
    Menelaus with the Body of Patroclus and the
    entrance arch in the background
    The sculptural group is a late 18th-century copy
    of an original from the 2nd century B.C.
    Marble. Height, 180 cm

6   North façade from the west colonnade of the
    main courtyard

7 Portico of the north façade

8 Lamps at the main entrance of the north façade
Early 19th century
Bronze

9 Lions adorning the portico of the west façade
Late 18th-century copies of antique originals
Marble. Length, 186 cm

Historical Sketch

The palace and park in Arkhangelskoye, a country estate of the eighteenth and nineteenth centuries situated 20 km from Moscow, so complement each other that it is difficult not to believe that the whole thing was, like a magic castle, conjured up out of thin air in an instant. In fact this architectural ensemble took fifty years to complete and forms what would be in archaeological terms simply the third "cultural stratum" in the history of the estate. The so-called *dyakovsky* site of a settlement built in the third or fourth century (still visible in the estate grounds) indicates that the banks of the Moskva have been inhabited since ancient times. It was on this site that the village of Upolozy grew. In the 1660s, the village wooden church (dating back to at least 1584) was replaced by one built in brick. The new church was consecrated to the Archangel Michael and the village was renamed Arkhangelskoye (Archangel in Russian is *Arkhangel*).

Although generally in the traditional mould of small churches found on Russian country estates, the low, whitewashed brick church in Arkhangelskoye does have rather an unusual composition. Russian architecture of the second half of the seventeenth century is typically decorative, using a variety of outlines and volumes to express itself. In the Arkhangelskoye church this is represented by the positioning of two small chapels one opposite the other on a diagonal which cuts across all three of the church's cupolas. Changes in practical requirements and the dictates of fashion have helped to shape this church. The rebuilding in 1848 was particularly important in this respect but work undertaken in the 1960s has largely restored it to its seventeenth-century appearance.

Situated on the steep river bank, this church with its low body (without the usual crypt), its onion cupola and its two side chapels, has undoubted charm. To the north of the church the archway, built in 1826 by Yevgraf Tiurin (1792–1870), faces the church's low, white stone porch with the carved portal. The window surrounds, the smooth sections of wall and the bands of relief stonework serve to lighten the heavy mass of the walls, above which the stone waves of the *kokoshniks** rise to the cupolas. Each façade has its own characteristic aspect.

The interior decoration of the church has not been preserved, but the original construction of the roof which survives is most interesting. The same kind of construction is to be found in the estate churches of Markovo and

---

* *Kokoshnik*: a purely decorative architectural feature semicircular in shape, often rising to a point (like the medieval Russian head-dress of the same name worn by married women) and framed by rich moulding.

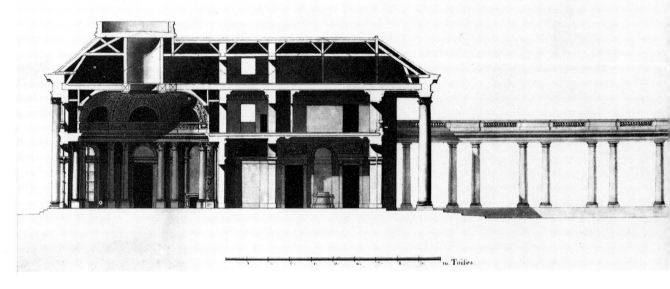

CHATEAU d'ARCANGELSKY.
Coupe sur la largeur.

The Arkhangelskoye Palace
Cross-section along the central axis. 1780
Designed by Charles de Guerne

Nikolskoye-Uriupino, near Moscow. These two villages and Arkhangelskoye belonged to the Princes Odoyevsky in the seventeenth century, and it is very likely that one and the same architect (possibly the serf Pavel Potekhin) was in charge of the construction of all three churches.

As was usual, the boyar's court was near the church. In Arkhangelskoye, this consisted of small log buildings with barns and outhouses. The Odoyevskys and, from 1681, the Cherkasskys rarely visited this little estate, and the boyar's court was usually occupied by the bailiff, who looked after the farms, the estate's only function at that time being to provide farm produce.

The first decade of the seventeenth century was the period when the famous reforms of Peter the Great were carried through and when the boyars' privileges were partially abolished and life in Russia was fundamentally changed. Innovations in Arkhangelskoye in the 1730s reflect this new era and are connected with the name of Prince Dmitry Golitsyn (1665–1737). Among the first of the Russian nobility to receive a European education Prince Dmitry was renowned as one of the greatest bibliophiles of Peter's time. The failure of his joint attempt with a number of other Russian nobles to limit the power of Empress Anna after Peter's death brought an end to his political career. From then on, the Prince's life was devoted to his books, in the quiet of his estate near Moscow. He began to construct a new estate in Arkhangelskoye, in accordance with the artistic canons

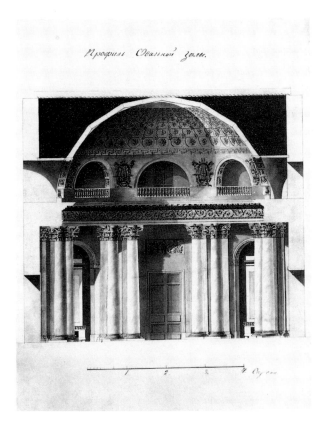

Cross-section of the Oval Hall. 1810s

of the Petrine epoch. A large wooden house was built at some distance from the church which thereby lost its position as the natural focal point of the estate. The house became Arkhangelskoye's centrepiece. Its south façade faced the Moskva River, with its windows looking out onto the avenues of a formal garden, laid out according to rules elaborated by the famous French landscape gardener André Lenotre. But the house and park were not yet a unified whole. The architecture of the estate showed features of the transitional style typical of the period when the new culture was taking its first tentative steps. Although traces of the old pre-Petrine tradition could be detected, it was already an elegant country estate, and its architecture and fittings show those artistic elements which later became classic features of most palace-and-park estates in Russia.

The building of the house and park was not yet finished. Forty years later Nikolai Golitsyn (1751–1809), grandson to Dmitry, regarded them as very old-fashioned. It is possible that the idea of completing the Arkhangelskoye estate came from his journey round the capitals of Europe and the impressions made on him by the country estates in France, Germany and Italy. At that time large landed estates were being built around Moscow. Many Russian nobles who were acquainted with European culture and had serf workmen under their command were trying to imitate tsars' country residences and at the same time were upholding their social status by building elegant estates and amassing works of art.

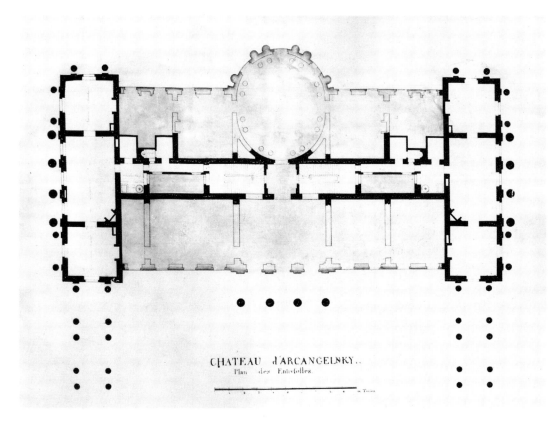

CHATEAU d'ARCANGELSKY..
Plan des Entresolles

The Arkhangelskoye Palace
Plan of the mezzanine. 1780
Designed by Charles de Guerne

The construction of the new Arkhangelskoye estate was begun in the last quarter of the eighteenth century. The domestic outbuildings with glasshouses on the steep bank of the Moskva were probably the first to be completed. At the beginning of the 1790s, terraces were raised in the park. On the uppermost terrace, where the wooden house had been, rose the brick walls of the palace. Pavilions and colonnades enclosing the main courtyard were added later. The few plans, sketches and draughts of that time give us little idea of the problems of construction, nor do they give us the name of the man behind a whole series of projects. It is certain that a number of architects took part in the work jointly creating a palace-and-park ensemble which became the model for formal estates built in the classical style.

We know the names of only three late eighteenth-century architects who were involved in the construction of this complex. The first was the French architect Charles de Guerne (1748–after 1789), whose signature is on the plan of the palace. The project was commissioned and completed in Paris in 1780 and it is unlikely that the architect visited Russia. The second architect, the Italian Giacomo Trombara (1742–1838), who designed the terraces in the park, came to Russia in 1799, and it was while he was working as a court architect in St Petersburg that he became acquainted with Prince Nikolai Golitsyn. To lay out a terraced park, the architect transformed the natural shape of the slope with great skill.

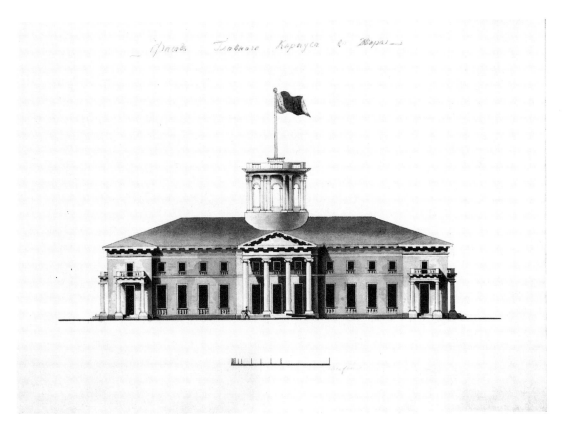

North façade of the Arkhangelskoye Palace. 1810s
Drawn by Vasily Strizhakov (?)

The breast-wall of the Lower Terrace, built by Trombara, was decorated with sculpture. The first statues appeared in Arkhangelskoye in the 1780s, and by 1810 there were over fifty sculptures in the park. They also adorned the pergolas and garden pavilions. One of these pavilions, the Library, was designed by Pettondi, about whom almost nothing is known. Beside the Library a small palace called Caprice was erected, and both buildings were known as the Caprice ensemble in the early nineteenth century.

A small ensemble, similar to the one in Arkhangelskoye and also named Caprice, is described by Derzhavin, a great Russian poet of the eighteenth century. His verses evoke the image of a country park with elegiac woods, flowering meadows and small hills.

But the park in Arkhangelskoye with its clipped trees and geometric plan of avenues corresponded little to the standards of landscape gardening current in the second part of the eighteenth century. From the 1770s onwards, the poetic and mysterious landscape garden (*jardin anglais*) began to replace the orderly and formal *jardin français*. However, the French garden did not entirely disappear: a small regular park was usually laid out before the house, and the rest of the area was taken up by a landscape park. In Arkhangelskoye, in comparison with other parks and gardens of that time, the regular part of the garden is unusually large and beautiful.

In 1810, the estate was bought by Prince Nikolai Yusupov (1751–1831). One of the richest men in Russia, Prince Yusupov received an excellent education and was renowned as an art-lover and connoisseur. From his retirement in 1804, the Prince lived in Moscow. He bought Arkhangelskoye, to house — in the palace and other buildings — his famous collection of paintings, numbering more than five hundred canvases, as well as marbles, bronzes, and terracottas.

Arkhangelskoye suffered extensive damage during the invasion of Russia in 1812 by Napoleon's army. Fortunately the bulk of the picture gallery and other collections were removed to safety. In the spring of 1813 repair work was begun on the palace and improvements were made on the estate. Prince Yusupov wanted to give it a more elegant and ceremonious aspect.

To this end he enlisted the leading Moscow architects Osip Beauvais (1784–1834) and Yevgraf Tiurin. Some of his own serfs acted as the architects' assistants. The best known of them was Vasily Strizhakov (1792–1819) who was foreman of work on the house. In 1817, he built the entrance archway, reminiscent of triumphal gates, to the design of Stepan Melnikov.

In 1818, the theatre was designed by Italian Pietro Gonzaga (1751–1831) and Osip Beauvais. The work was carried out by the Vladimir team of carpenters under the supervision of the architects Tiurin, Melnikov, and Strizhakov. It is a modest building with plain walls and a small portico. The simplicity of the exterior is contrasted with the sumptuous auditorium. The low walls are attractively painted to imitate stone rustication. A two-tier arcade accommodates boxes lined with blue velvet, and the powerful pillars of imitation marble lend elegance to the hall. Probably the best view of the hall is from the stage. The theatre was the only architectural project Pietro Gonzaga realized in his life.

The fire of 1820 destroyed almost completely the furnishing of the palace. The picture gallery and other collections were saved but the whole palace had to be completely redecorated. The architect Yevgraf Tiurin and the painter Nicolas de Courteille (1768– after 1830) were put in charge of the work, which was completed at the end of the 1820s. At that time, when many of the famous estates around Moscow were in decline, Arkhangelskoye, with its picture gallery, theatre, porcelain factory, glasshouses and botanic garden, struck visitors as a remnant of the eighteenth century. "Crossing your threshold, I am suddenly carried into the days of Catherine," wrote the great Russian poet Alexander Pushkin, who visited Arkhangelskoye in 1827 and in 1830. The decline of the estate began in the 1830s, after the death of the old prince. The best paintings and sculptures were transferred to the Yusupovs' Petersburg palace. The orchestra and the company of actors were disbanded, and the rare plants of the famous botanic garden were sold.

That the large formal estates were in general decline was simply a sign of the socio-economic crisis in Russia. From the 1830s till the end of the century, no construction work took place in Arkhangelskoye. Only in the years 1909–16 was

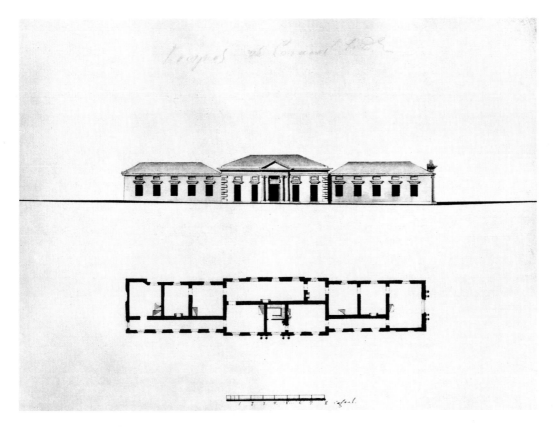

Façade and plan of the Small Palace (The Caprice). 1810s

a large mausoleum, known as the Colonnade, built by Roman Klein (1858–1924) in the estate grounds. The decoration of the domed hall in this building was carried out by Ignaty Nivinsky (1881–1933).

After the October Revolution Arkhangelskoye was turned into a museum.

The visitor approaches the ensemble by the broad drive that leads to the palace. Gradually the pediment and arch of the gateway come into view at the end of the vast green corridor and behind the gates, through the wrought iron, can be seen the columns of the palace portico in front of which is a forecourt surrounded by white colonnades.

The eloquent simplicity and severe clarity of line typical of Russian classical architecture is particularly fine in the palace of Arkhangelskoye. The general rhythm is effected by the alternating orders and dimensions of the columns. The imposing Tuscan columns of the entrance arch harmonize beautifully with the white-stone colonnades forming a spacious forecourt, the thirty-foot-high Ionic columns of the palace central portico and the light Corinthian columns of the palace belvedere.

A magnificent vista spreads out from the south façade: a strict pattern of marble figures, and open-work balustrades sloping down to woods on the horizon. Although the formal park is not large (around 14 hectares), it gives the impression of a vast area.

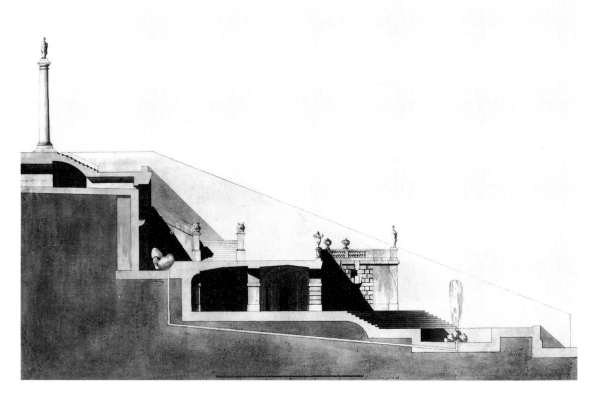

Cross-section of the park terraces. Late 18th century
Designed by Giacomo Trombara (?)

The Upper Terrace of the park is similar in dimensions to the foreyard, but here the fusion of nature and architecture is more evident. Mirroring the white line of the colonnades on the north side, a row of giant larches can be seen extending towards the palace and forming a background against which the severely classical herms stand out clearly. The boundary of the Upper Terrace is marked by a balustrade on which marble vases stand, and a stairway cuts through its centre. Decorated by sculptures the stairway catches the eye from a distance.

The Lower Terrace, with the round bowl of a fountain in the centre, runs parallel to the façade of the palace. Here the low-cut lawns are replaced by glades of birch and fir. This gradual transition to the landscape park makes the Lower Terrace a picturesque and poetic spot for the visitor. The stairway of the Lower Terrace, leading to the parterre, descends in two flights of steps to the foot of the breast-wall. The many busts on this wall are turned towards the parterre which is bound by old, trimmed lime-trees and decked with marble statues.

Sculpture plays a significant role in Arkhangelskoye. It is difficult to imagine this magnificent ensemble without its two hundred decorative statues. They are the work of Russian and foreign sculptors of the eighteenth and early nineteenth centuries. No other country estate near Moscow can boast such a wealth of statuary. The statues not only embellish the palace and park, they also serve as a perspective terminal point for many avenues.

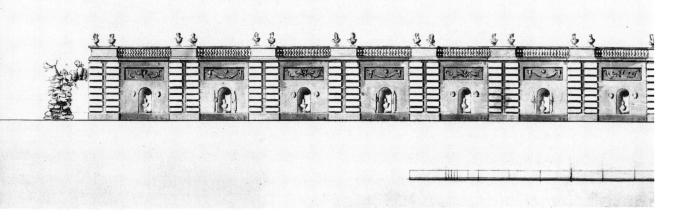

The Lower Terrace. Western part of the breast-wall. 1810s

As well as sculptures, there are many pergolas and pavilions in the park. Among the towering pines are the white columns of the Memorial to Catherine, which is at the end of one of the main axial avenues of the park. This little pergola, designed as a memorial to Catherine II, is graced with a bronze figure of Themis, goddess of justice, and is a copy of the work of the Russian sculptor Mikhail Kozlovsky (1753–1802). From the Memorial can be seen the pavilion which was named the Tea House in the nineteenth century. It is part of the old Library pavilion that survived the fire of 1829. The beautiful design of the cornice, the very delicate stuccowork on the turquoise ceiling, and the light columns around the walls of the small rotunda hall, lend special beauty to the building. Beside it is the Caprice, rebuilt in the Empire style in the 1820s. Its façades were restored by Soviet architects. This building looks very striking from a distance. Five lines of avenues separate the Caprice from the parterre. Each of them is intersected by smaller paths, so that when the visitor walks along these paths he sees now memorial columns of grey marble, now the expressive silhouettes of vases and sculptures, now the gilt walls and white columns of the Caprice itself. Looking from the south, from the edge of the parterre, we have another magnificent view of the ensemble: the great expanse of green and the white walls of the terraces topped by balustrades decorated with sculptures. Over all this the palace rises in a frame of larch-trees.

25

At the main entrance to the palace is the elegant portico. The broad, glazed doors lead from the porch into the Vestibule which in turn leads into the central suite of rooms of the palace. With its strict verticals of imitation marble pilasters, its silver-grey walls and ceiling painted to imitate stuccowork, the Vestibule is given an air of formal solemnity and at the same time prepares the visitor for the inner apartments of the palace.

The interior, refitted after the fire of 1820 in the late classical style, consists of state apartments on the ground floor and more modest rooms on the first floor, including the library and living quarters, whose decor and furniture have not survived.

With the exception of the Vestibule, Antechamber and Oval Hall, the wall and ceiling ornamentation plays only a minor role in the general scheme of decoration in the state rooms, and is sometimes reminiscent of a picture frame.

Situated in the centre of the palace, the Oval Hall, with its two tiers of windows, is the largest and most magnificent chamber. Coupled columns of imitation marble around the walls support the moulded entablatures. Above them, the gallery pierced with arches extends round the entire hall which is crowned with a cupola painted to imitate caissons. The wealth of light, the many mirrors, the predominance of gold in the paintings, the amber glimmer of the parquet, poplar and Karelian birchwood furniture, the great gilt chandelier — all these are effectively combined with the moulded details of the capitals, entablatures and the balustrade of the gallery.

On either side of the Oval Hall are suites of state rooms, each one similar in design. The silver-grey, greenish or pale-blue stretches of walls are decorated by friezes. The ceiling paintings are of subdued colours; the pattern of the parquet is repeated in two or three variants. The concise artistic language, typical of late classicism, emphasizes the stylistic unity and gives an impression of wholeness. Yet at the same time these state apartments are striking in their variety and in their wealth of everchanging effects.

Unlike the Imperial Room, formal and hung with portraits of Russian emperors, the State Bedroom impresses with its refined blue tonality and silvered furniture. The alcove with its carved bed is marked off by four white pillars.

Next is a smallish octagonal room whose piers are decorated with panels by Hubert Robert (1733–1808), all of equal dimension and depicting majestic ruins. This room opens the west suite of rooms consisting of two octagonal Hubert Robert rooms, linked by the Antique Gallery. These three rooms form a single whole. The Hubert Robert rooms, reminiscent of lanterns, look out onto the park. The birds and bouquets in the paintings, the flowers in mahogany jardinières, landscapes by Robert, with their churches and statues overgrown with green, together with views of the real park beyond the windows — all these give the impression of a harmonious unity and a natural link between the palace and surrounding nature.

Anonymous artist
The Main Street in the Village of Arkhangelskoye. 1820s
Oil on cardboard. 28 × 46 cm

The Antique Gallery is decorated with representations of griffins, vases, shields and other attributes of antiquity framed by silvery ornaments. On the flat ceiling are painted vaults with caissons. In the room are a few antique sculptures of the first to the third centuries and many eighteenth- and nineteenth-century copies of antique originals.

The Tiepolo Room, one of the largest rooms in the palace, next claims attention. Like the Second Hubert Robert Room, it was rebuilt in 1816 by the serf architect Strizhakov. Here are placed two vast canvases by Giovanni Battista Tiepolo (1696–1770), which once hung opposite the windows, extending the space and making the hall seem even bigger.

Two state rooms — the Saloon (The Cupid Room) and the Study — are situated in the south suite of the palace, both decorated with rosettes, lyres and swans framed by garlands of flowers. They are painted in a greenish-grey typical of the 1820s. In the Saloon, however, the Empire style wall paintings do not at first seem to be in harmony with the elegant gilt furniture of the 1790s. The probable explanation is that the taste of the owner of the estate lay in the eighteenth century: he valued the artistic qualities of the older things and was in no hurry to change the carved and gilt suite of Catherine's time for fashionable Empire furniture. The restrained range of colours in the wall painting, the subdued shades of the carpets and the faded golden upholstery of the chairs form a background for the main decorations of the interior: paintings by French masters of the seventeenth and eighteenth centuries.

In both rooms, the Saloon and the Study, paintings play a very important part. In the Study, for instance, 35 canvases completely cover the walls, leaving space for only a painted frieze whose design matches the decorative details of the Russian furniture of poplar and Karelian birch.

In the Saloon, in accordance with the tastes current in the late eighteenth century, gilt furniture is placed only along the walls. The Study, on the other hand, is typical of a sitting-room of the 1820s with settees, armchairs and tables arranged in groups seeming to invite the guest to rest and conversation. Here, too, are the Viennese piano and the lady's writing table, possibly of French make. The pictures in the Study are for the most part by Flemish and Dutch artists; although there are some seascapes and portraits of the French school and some Italian landscapes. The unusual decorative richness of the Study makes it one of the most pleasing rooms of the palace.

Adjoining the Study are three small "winter" rooms, the former living quarters. In the 1830s, many head studies by the Italian painter Pietro Antonio Rotari (1707–1762) were hung in the First Winter Room, which was at that time a bedroom. The original decoration of the Second Winter Room has not been preserved. The Third Winter Room contains Russian furniture of the nineteenth century. It is upholstered in silk, which may have been manufactured by the serf craftsmen of Prince Yusupov's workshop in the village of Kupavna near Moscow. Here are bookcases and family portraits in gilt frames. In 1978, a doorway which had been blocked up in the middle of the last century, was reopened, giving access from the Third Winter Room to the State Dining-room. The latter is a vast hall painted in the Egyptian style, with musicians' galleries and a pantry. Colourful cabinets with Chinese porcelain, cases displaying ceramics produced by local serf craftsmen, a huge canvas painted by Gabriel-François Doyen (1726–1806) in the late eighteenth century, a portrait of the young Prince Boris Yusupov in an exotic tartar garb by Antoine Jean Gros (1771–1835) — this wealth of objects of various times and styles is typical of the Russian palace interior of the 1830s.

The wooden staircase, painted to resemble marble and built in 1817 to Melnikov's design, leads to the Library on the first floor. In comparison with the state apartments on the ground floor, the rooms of the Library, with their simple pine floors, are not large. The walls are painted in soft shades of green, blue and cream, and there are very few sculptures and paintings. In the mahogany bookcases lining the walls the spines of old books gleam — sixteen thousand volumes ranging from incunabula of the late fifteenth century to editions from the first quarter of the last century. In these rooms there is an atmosphere of calm and concentration. A selection of furniture of the first third of the nineteenth century is to be found here: armchairs, banquettes, various tables, corner sofas as well as

Nicolas de Courteille (1768–after 1830)
Festive Day in Arkhangelskoye. 1830
A copy of the original housed in the All-Union
Pushkin Museum, Pushkin
Pencil and watercolour. 40.5 × 52.6 cm

several interesting lamps, including oil lamps of intricate forms. Arkhangelskoye
is one of the few estates around Moscow that still has a library dating from the
early nineteenth century.

Among the palace's artistic collections the picture gallery arouses great
interest. Its basis is the collection of Western European works from the seventeenth to the first half of the nineteenth centuries. Today it is not as great as it was
a century and a half ago: many first-class canvases were transferred to the Hermitage in Leningrad and to the Pushkin Museum of Fine Arts in Moscow; yet the
Arkhangelskoye picture gallery still holds masterpieces.

The small collection of seventeenth-century Dutch paintings includes *The
Skirmish* by Philips Wouwerman (1619–1683), *Still Life with Fruit* by Jan
Davidsz de Heem (1606–1683), *Night Landscape* by Aert van der Neer
(1607–1677), *The Adoration of the Magi* by Leonaert Bramer (1596–1674),
works by Jan Both (*ca* 1618–1652), Karel Du Jardin (1622–1678) and Nicolaes
Berchem (1620–1683). An excellent example of seventeenth-century Flemish
paintings is the *Portrait of a Lady* by Anthony van Dyck (1599–1641). The image
is exceptionally fine, the execution is brilliant, and the colouring refined. Of the
other painters of the school of Rubens particular mention should be made of
Abraham van Diepenbeeck (1596–1675), who painted the large-scale allegorical
canvas *Minerva Protecting Fertility from Mars*. Here, too, is the picture entitled

The Battle by Karel Breydel (1678–1733), the Flemish painter of battle scenes. The pride of the picture gallery are two canvases by the outstanding eighteenth-century Venetian painter, Giovanni Battista Tiepolo. His *Meeting of Antony and Cleopatra* and *Cleopatra's Feast*, produced in the middle of the eighteenth century, display the particular features of his painting — a brilliant mastery of composition, his painterly gift and his rich use of colour. Following the traditions of the great Venetian artists of the Renaissance, Tiepolo depicts himself among the characters portrayed in *Cleopatra's Feast*. Prince Yusupov bought these paintings from an Italian dealer, who had brought them to St Petersburg.

The gallery also has paintings by other eighteenth-century Italian masters: Jacopo Amigoni (1682–1752), Francesco Tironi (died 1800), Pompeo Girolamo Batoni (1708–1787) and Pietro Antonio Rotari.

French painting is more widely and variously represented in the Arkhangelskoye picture gallery. Among the works of the seventeenth century are a landscape by Claude Lorraine (1600–1682) and a picture by Jean Tassaile (1608–1667), *Iphigenia Brought to Sacrifice*. A Flemish-born flower painter Jean-Baptiste Monnoyer (1636–1699) is represented by the magnificent *Still Life*. Also of interest is a small painting by François Boucher (1703–1770), *The Startled Bather*, a typical example of rococo court art. In the middle of the eighteenth century this painting belonged to Mme de Pompadour. The collection of French art of the second half of the eighteenth century is especially large. It is possible to follow almost the entire artistic career of the remarkable painter of marines, Claude Joseph Vernet (1714–1789), from his canvases displayed in the Arkhangelskoye gallery. The gallery has twelve paintings by Hubert Robert, who was very popular in the eighteenth century. Most of them decorate the two Hubert Robert rooms.

Among paintings on themes of ancient history and mythology, so popular in the seventeenth and eighteenth centuries, are two large canvases by Gabriel-François Doyen, *Andromache Protecting Astyanax* and *The Triumph of Claudius*. At the turn of the eighteenth and nineteenth centuries many French artists came to Russia, among them Marie Anne Elisabeth Vigée-Lebrun (1755–1842), who painted the portraits of Countess Maria Kochubei and the Italian operatic soprano Angelica Catalani. At almost the same time as Vigée-Lebrun, Jean Laurent Mosnier (1743–1808) worked in Russia, and he painted a portrait of the estate owner's wife, Princess Tatyana Yusupova.

The picture gallery in Arkhangelskoye was one of the few collections in Russia to display works by Jacques-Louis David (1748–1825), the great master of the time of the French Revolution, and by artists of his school. At the beginning of the nineteenth century David's painting *Sappho and Phaon*, commissioned by Prince Nikolai Yusupov, hung in this gallery. It is now housed in the Hermitage, Leningrad. The Prince also acquired several paintings of David's school, such as the *Vow of the Horatii* by Armand-Charles Caraffe (1762–1822) and *Theseus and*

Cross-section of the Arkhangelskoye Theatre. 1817 (?)

Peirithous by Angelica Mongez (1775–1855). Other noteworthy works by French artists are the companion canvases by Charles Amédée Philippe van Loo (1719–1795), *The Bouquet* by Jean Louis Prévost (1760–1810), and *Cupid and Psyche* by the little-known artist Bernard de Niort active at the end of the eighteenth century.

In the first quarter of the eighteenth century a number of artists worked in Russia who, although not particularly famous, are very interesting in their own way. In the palace picture gallery their work is represented by a series of paintings by Nicolas de Courteille, who lived in Moscow for many years and often worked in Arkhangelskoye, and also by the genre scenes of Russian life by Jacques François Swebach (1769–1823) and his son Bernard Édouard Swebach (1800–1870).

Even this short list of the most significant works of the Italian, French and Dutch school (there are very few paintings from other schools in Arkhangelskoye) gives an idea of the character of the picture gallery built up over a half century from the 1770s. By the 1820s it had become one of the largest private collections in Russia and one which well illustrates the taste of a Russian noble who had spent years in Western Europe. There are very few works by Russian painters in Prince Yusupov's collection: the most interesting of them are a portrait of Emperor Paul I by Stepan Shchukin (1762–1828), *A View of St Petersburg* by

Fiodor Alexeyev (1753–1824), and a small painting by Alexander Orlovsky (1777–1832), *The Horseman*. Along with the names of well-known Russian artists we should note several local serf artists, Fiodor Sotnikov, Mikhail Poltev, Yegor Shebanin, Ivan Kolesnikov and Grigory Novikov. They taught their pupils at the School of Art founded in Arkhangelskoye in 1818. The serf artists painted porcelain, copied drawings and in the 1820s made illustrated catalogues of the picture gallery and the collection of park sculptures and bronzes.

These unique catalogues became part of the gallery's collection of drawings, which contains more than a thousand sheets. Its most valuable part is a small selection of drawings by such outstanding artists as Jacopo Bassano, Pietro Gonzaga, Giovanni Domenico Tiepolo, Jacob Jordaens and Hubert Robert.

The state apartments of the palace are beautifully furnished. Some of the furniture was made in St Petersburg to the designs of famous architects, and some was copied in various workshops. A series of articles was made by serf craftsmen. Among the first-class products of furniture-makers of the early classical period are white suites with gilt details (1790s) in the Imperial Room, and similar, though possibly earlier, pieces of gilt furniture in the Antique Gallery, whose splendid carved mirror frames were probably made at the Moscow workshop of Pavel Spol.

The furniture of the State Bedroom was made possibly by Baltic craftsmen in the last quarter of the eighteenth century. The restored upholstery, of patterned blue damask, is a copy of the Lyon silk it replaces.

The Saloon's light and elegant carved furniture from the late eighteenth century is also upholstered in a golden damask imitating the original. Painted and gilt furniture was going out of fashion at the turn of the eighteenth and nineteenth centuries, and poplar and Karelian birch furniture attained wide popularity in Russia. In the Oval Hall, the Study and the Third Winter Room there are magnificent suites of furniture made of Karelian birch in the first quarter of the nineteenth century. The large mahogany suites in the Tiepolo Room were produced in the 1830s. At roughly the same time, serf craftsmen made the white painted tables with gilt stars that are in the Second Hubert Robert Room. Here, too, is the table painted with garlands of flowers. Throughout the palace are also to be found various pieces of furniture made by foreign craftsmen.

The crystal, bronze and gilt wood chandeliers are completely in tune with the formal character of the palace. The huge, three-tier chandelier in the Oval Hall was made by Russian craftsmen in the 1820s. Various candlesticks and sconces of black bronze and ormolu, girandoles hung with prisms, ornamental lamps and candelabra (two bronze candelabra bearing the signature of the famous French craftsman Pierre-Philippe Tomire, 1751–1843, are specially noteworthy) decorate the palace.

An important role in interior design was played by porcelain: Chinese and Japanese vases, porcelain flowers, crockery and services. Besides articles pro-

Part of a tea service
The Yusupov Porcelain Workshop in Arkhangelskoye
Painted by a serf artist. 1820s
Porcelain

duced by various Russian and European factories there are items from the Arkhangelskoye Porcelain Workshop (1818–39). Here white porcelain articles bought from factories at home and abroad were painted by serf artists. This porcelain, with the mark "Arkhangelskoye", hardly ever went on sale: small sets of separate articles were made as presentation pieces for visiting members of the Tsar's family or for other important guests. Porcelain articles are usually painted with flowers, fruit, birds and butterflies. But of special interest are articles decorated with copies of paintings and engravings from Prince Yusupov's collection. There are, for instance, copies of paintings by Jean-Baptiste Greuze (1725–1805), Louis Léopold Boilly (1761–1845), Pietro Antonio Rotari and Marie Anne Élisabeth Vigée-Lebrun, of engravings by Jacques François Swebach and of lithographs by Ivan Semionov. Intricate faience vessels produced at Arkhangelskoye were made from Gzhel clay, renowned for its special quality (Gzhel was a small town in Moscow province).

Among Arkhangelskoye's most important artistic treasures are the curtain and four backdrops by Pietro Gonzaga. When Prince Yusupov was the Russian envoy in Turin at the end of the eighteenth century, he invited Gonzaga to Russia. From 1818 till 1825 this remarkable artist, working in Moscow and St Petersburg, painted ten backdrops and a curtain for the Arkhangelskoye theatre. Even then the theatre was, first and foremost, a show-case for Gonzaga's scen-

Dish
The Yusupov Porcelain Workshop in Arkhangelskoye
Painted by a serf artist. 1820s
Porcelain. Diam. 23.3 cm

ery. We know nothing about the performances staged in this theatre, although the serf company often performed in Prince Yusupov's Moscow theatre. From memoirs of his contemporaries we know that the owner of Arkhangelskoye treasured these stage-sets. Instead of the fashionable ballets, operas and vaudevilles, he occasionally displayed the famous artist's scenery to the accompaniment of music. Gonzaga's stage-sets struck the viewer with their unusual perspective and the seeming reality of their churches, palaces and dungeons. For this artist, who throughout his long life designed stage-sets for many theatres in Italy and Russia, the small stage in Arkhangelskoye became a place where he, with the support of the estate owner, could realize his idea of immortalizing his art in "shows of scenery". Such shows were staged in Arkhangelskoye until the death of Prince Yusupov. Today the Arkhangelskoye theatre is the only place where one can see backdrops by this celebrated Italian theatrical artist. There is also a curtain depicting a magnificent hall with gilt chandeliers and columns of porphyry. Behind it is the first of the surviving backdrops: the gloomy, dark vaults of a prison. You have only to lift the truncated arch and backdrop of the Prison and the elegant colonnade of a magnificent Roman Temple is revealed. The next stage-set, the Malachite Hall, depicts a vast pillared hall with a pinkish vault and gilt statuary. The receding perspective creates an impression of great distance, and it is hard to believe that it fits into the twelve-metre width of the

Dish
The Yusupov Porcelain Workshop in Arkhangelskoye
Painted by a serf artist. 1820s
Porcelain. Diam. 23.3 cm

stage. The last surviving backcloth shows a tavern with a mass of detail — down to a cat with holes for eyes: a lamp hung behing the backdrop would give them movement and sparkle. We can obtain an impression of the missing Gonzaga stage-sets from watercolours by serf artists, which are still in Arkhangelskoye.

More than sixty years have passed since that day in May, 1919, when the Arkhangelskoye Palace Museum was opened to the public. In the first four years alone it received some twenty thousand visitors. Soon after the museum was created, a systematic stock-taking and description of the artistic collections was begun. From the end of the 1920s the task of stock-taking and description grew considerably with the return of works which had been removed from the estate in the nineteenth century. Among them were canvases by Giovanni Battista Tiepolo, Anthony van Dyck, Gabriel-François Doyen, François Boucher and other artists. The collection of drawings, porcelain and ceramics was enlarged. All this made possible the restoration of the palace interior to its 1820s appearance and the organization of interesting exhibitions.

To preserve the Arkhangelskoye ensemble and its collection, restoration work was carried out (1924–29) on breast-walls and balustrades in the park, and on the parquet, the wall painting and the pictures in the palace. Restoration of the paintings was done by such noted artists as Pavel and Alexander Korin, Vasily Yakovlev, Stepan Churakov. In 1934–40, the Theatre was restored.

In the war years (1941–45), Arkhangelskoye suffered from repeated Nazi air raids. The park sculpture was buried and the other collections were removed to the Urals in October, 1941. Three years later they were brought back to Arkhangelskoye. By the end of 1945 the ground floor exhibition had already been partially restored, and in one room was organized an exhibition of rare books to mark the 150th anniversary of the birth of Pushkin.

During the ten years following the war, major restoration of the palace, painting, sculpture and furniture took place. In the mid-fifties Arkhangelskoye was reopened to the public and now the museum receives more than four hundred thousand visitors annually.

Between 1966 and 1980 restoration work had been done on the Church of the Archangel Michael, the Yusupov Mausoleum, the Theatre, the Caprice, and the bailiff's house (the office wing).

The museum has scientific and artistic links with the most important museums in the USSR and with their help organizes exhibitions of ancient Russian art, architectural drawings, ceramics and portraits. At present a new cycle of restoration is taking place in Arkhangelskoye — a sign that this remarkable memorial will live for ages to come.

The Palace

11 The Vestibule *(pls. 11–13)*
Sculptural group: *Castor and Pollux*
A late 18th-century copy of an antique original
Marble. Height, 176 cm

14 The Oval Hall *(pls. 14–18)*
South part of the hall with French windows
looking onto the park

15 Musicians' gallery
Ceiling painting: *Cupid and Psyche*. 1820s
By Nicolas de Courteille
Oil on canvas. 200 × 300 cm

16 Chandelier. Detail
By Viglin (?). Russia. 1830s
Mixture of chalk, glue and drying oil,
hardened and gilt

7   Capitals and entablature of the columns. 1820s
    By Semion Merkulov and Ivan Lazarev

18   Wall painting: *Allegory of Painting*. 1820s
     Detail
     Grisaille

The Imperial Room *(pls. 19–21)*
Suite of rooms in the west part of the palace

20 Two candelabra and clock on the mantelshelf
France. Late 18th or early 19th century
Marble and ormolu

21   Girandole
Russia. Mid-18th century
Cut glass and ormolu

22   The State Bedroom *(pls. 22, 23)*

26 Statue of a Boy
Ancient Rome. 2nd or 3rd century
Marble. Height, 89 cm

29 The Tiepolo Room *(pls. 29–33)*
View of the room from the Vestibule. On the
wall opposite, *The Meeting of Antony and
Cleopatra* (1747) by Giovanni Battista Tiepolo
(1696–1770)
Oil on canvas. 333 × 603 cm

30 Giovanni Battista Tiepolo. 1696–1770
The Meeting of Antony and Cleopatra. 1747
Detail

31   Giovanni Battista Tiepolo. 1696–1770
     Cleopatra's Feast. 1740s
     Oil on canvas. 338 × 606 cm

32 View of the room from the Second Hubert
Robert Room

33 Giovanni Battista Tiepolo. 1696–1770
Cleopatra's Feast. 1740s. Detail with a self-
portrait (between pillars)

34 The Saloon (The Cupid Room) *(pls. 34, 35)*
Fireside screen. Russia. 1780s
Carved and gilt wood
Jean-Louis Prévost the Younger. 1760–1810
Vase of Flowers. 1787
Oil on canvas. 101 × 76 cm

35 Candelabrum
Russia. Late 18th or early 19th century
Porcelain and ormolu

37   Anthony van Dyck. 1599–1641
Portrait of a Lady. 1630s
Oil on canvas. 205 × 120 cm

38 Jardinière
France (?). Late 18th or early 19th century
Mahogany, painted porcelain and ormolu

40 Settee
Russia. 1800–25
Carved poplar, painted and gilt

41 Back of an armchair. 1800–25
Carved poplar, painted and gilt

42 The Rotari Room (The First Winter Room)
(*pls. 42–45*)
View of the room from the Inter-communicating
Room

43 South-west part of the room

44   Pietro Rotari. 1707–1762
Peasant Girl under a Tree. 1750s–1760s
Oil on canvas. 106 × 84 cm

45 Pietro Rotari. 1707–1762
Old Woman. 1750s–1760s
Oil on canvas. 43 × 33 cm

46 The Prince's Study (The Third Winter Room)
(pls. 46–49)
View of the study from the Inter-communicating
Room

47 Clock: *Hector's Farewell to Andromache*
France. 1800–25
Marble and ormolu

48 Decorated door of a sideboard
Russia. 1820s
Karelian birch, walnut and ormolu

49 Writing desk
Russia. Early 19th century
Poplar and water-seasoned oak, carved and gilt

52 Sideboard
Russia
Oak
Ceramic panel
England. Pottery Works of Josiah Wedgwood.
Late 18th century

53 Stand with vases
China. Late 18th or early 19th century
Porcelain

56 Charles Amédée Philippe van Loo. 1719–1795
Electricity Experiment. 1777
Oil on canvas. 115 × 88 cm

The Park

57 Herms adorning the central path of the Upper
Terrace. Early 19th century
Marble

58 Fountain of the Lower Terrace viewed from the Upper Terrace

59 *Hercules and Anteus*. Second half of the 18th century
Enlarged copy of a 17th-century terracotta by Stefano Maderno done after Michelangelo's original
Marble. Height, 200 cm

60 Central part of the Lower Terrace and the
Large Parterre from the Upper Terrace

61 Sculptures adorning the balustrade of the Lower
Terrace

63   Balustrade of the Upper Terrace and the south
façade of the Palace from the Lower Terrace

64 Fountain: *Cupids with Dolphins*. 1889
By Giromello
Marble. Height, 160 cm

73 The Pink Fountain Pergola. 1850s
Cupid with a Swan (intended for a fountain).
Second half of the 18th century
Marble. Height, 115 cm

74 The Library (The Tea House).
East façade. 1834
Designed by Vasily Dregalov

75 The Small Palace (The Caprice)
Portico of the east façade. 1819
Designed by Yevgraf Tiurin

76 The Holy Gates. 1824
    Designed by Yevgraf Tiurin

77 The Stone Store Room by the Ravine
    Designed by an unknown 18th-century
    architect. Rebuilt in 1826 by Osip Beauvais

78 The Yusupov Mausoleum. 1909–16
Designed by Roman Klein

79 Colonnade of the Yusupov Mausoleum

80 The picé wall at the Church of the Archangel
Michael. 1826
Designed by Yevgraf Tiurin

81 Church of the Archangel Michael. 1660s
View from the west

82, 83 Church of the Archangel Michael
View from the east

The Theatre

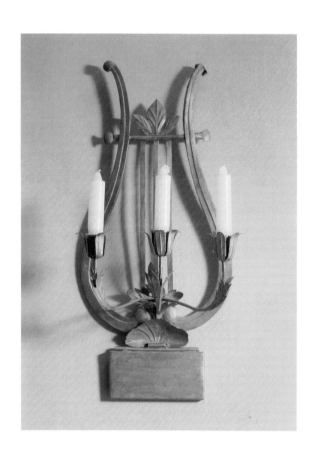

85 South façade of the Theatre. 1817–18
Designed by Pietro Gonzaga and Osip Beauvais

88 Pietro Gonzaga. 1751–1831
The Temple. Stage-set design. 1810s
Watercolour. 25.4 × 35 cm

89 Pietro Gonzaga. 1751–1831
The Tavern. Stage-set design. 1810s
Watercolour. 32 × 43 cm

90   *The Malachite Hall.* Copy of a stage-set design
by Pietro Gonzaga. 1830s
Watercolour. 37.5 × 52 cm

91   Nicolas de Courteille. 1768– after 1830
Portrait of a Serf Actress (?). 1820s
Coloured pencil and lacquer. 55 × 41 cm

92 Nicolas de Courteille. 1768– after 1830
Portrait of a Serf Actress (?). 1820s
Coloured pencil and lacquer. 58 × 43 cm

93   *The Roman Temple.* Copy of a stage-set design
by Pietro Gonzaga. 1830s
Watercolour. 28.5 × 36.5 cm

94 *The Prison.* Copy of a stage-set design by Pietro
Gonzaga. 1830s
Watercolour. 27 × 43 cm

Nicolas de Courteille. 1768– after 1830
Portrait of the Serf Actress Anna Borunova. 1821
Oil on canvas. 131 × 93 cm

Annotations

The Palace

The palace was built in the 1790s after the design of the French architect Charles de Guerne (1748– after 1789), although the original plan was modified during construction. The building itself is made of plastered brick but the socle, portico columns and colonnades of the main courtyard are of white stone. The central part of the main north façade is a tall tetrastyle portico. The early classical exterior of the building has been preserved almost intact. Only the decorative balusters from the niches below the windows of the ground and first floor and the coping stones from the balconies over the small porticos on the south and side façades have been lost.

The interior decoration of the palace, the painting of the façades and the construction of the colonnades was completed in 1812. However in the same year the palace was severely damaged during Napoleon's invasion of Russia; it was restored in 1813–15 under the supervision of the architects Osip Beauvais and Ilya Zhukov, and the serf mason Vasily Strizhakov. In 1817, the belvedere, built in 1814, was reconstructed.

In 1813–14, the west pavilion of the main courtyard, which had housed a theatre and living quarters in the Golitsyns' time, was converted into a picture gallery and library. The work was carried out by Zhukov and Strizhakov. In 1815, Strizhakov built a passage over the colonnade from the palace to the library. The balusters bounding the passage were designed by Beauvais.

In 1817, the entrance archway to the main courtyard was built by Stepan Melnikov. Probably at that time the pavilions were enlarged to adjoin the arch, and their façades on the side of the courtyard were concealed by semicircular brick walls (screens) pierced with entry arches that led into small inner courts. The wrought-iron gates of the main entry and the gates to the inner courts, with their gilded bronze details, were made at the beginning of the nineteenth century and installed in Arkhangelskoye in the 1900s. In the 1920s, winged figures symbolizing glory were painted over the gateway on both sides of the main arch. At the same time the screen walls of the courtyard were also painted to represent colonnades with a green park behind it. These paintings were restored in 1934. In 1946, new paintings representing colonnades and the Muses took their place. The paintwork of the entrance arch was restored in 1965.

In 1830, the sculpture *Menelaus with the Body of Patroclus*, a late eighteenth-century copy of an ancient original, was placed in the centre of the main courtyard.

The palace was badly damaged by fire in 1820. It was repaired under the supervision of Tiurin and the assistant architect Vasily Alexandrov. In 1820, Osip Ivanov's team of workers re-erected the belvedere on the roof of the palace, making it slightly higher this time. Significant repairs to the palace were carried out in 1857 under the serf architect Piotr Shestakov. In Soviet times the walls and roof have often been repaired, the façade repainted, and the old stone blocks replaced by new ones. In 1933–37, the palace pavilions were altered, as a result of which the shape of the windows was changed and the interior decor lost. At the same time the glasshouses on the southern limit of the regular garden were replaced by new buildings in the style of the first quarter of the nineteenth century. The years 1951–54 saw major restoration of the palace.

The Vestibule

Three glass doors lead from the porch into the Vestibule, a large square room with corners slightly rounded by concave pilasters. Other pilasters divide each wall of the Vestibule into three equal parts, in each of which is either a door, or an archway or else a niche with a fireplace or a sculpture. There are ten doors and archways in this room. The archways, glazed in the mid-nineteenth century, flank the door leading, through the Antechamber, to the Oval Hall; the door on the left-hand side opens into the Tiepolo Room, the one on the right-hand side, into the State Dining-room; and besides, there are two false doors supposedly leading to the two latter rooms, and, finally, three doors lead onto the porch. The ceiling, walls, pilasters and demicolumns are plastered. The ceiling and walls were painted by Nicolas de Courteille, Colombius (Colombo), Rungi and their assistants after the 1820 fire. Under Courteille's supervision they also painted all the other rooms of the palace. The stucco detail is the work of Ivan Lazarev.

The Vestibule looks today as it did in the 1820s except that in place of the marble dogs there were figures of gladiators — Paolo Triscorni's copies of ancient originals. The 1820s chandelier, made of gilt wood and hardened mixture of chalk, clay and drying oil by an unknown Russian craftsman, is also still there.

The Antechamber

The small, square Antechamber is decorated with Corinthian demicolumns. Corinthian columns stand on either side of the doors leading to the main staircase. The motifs and colours in the painting of the Antechamber follow those of the Vestibule. The Antechamber can be entered from four sides: from the Vestibule, the Oval Hall and from the two landings of the staircase. The wooden stair painted to imitate marble, with flights leading off on either side of the Antechamber, was built in 1817 to the design of Melnikov and was rebuilt after the fire of 1820 by the team of Osip Ivanov.

Each landing at the top of the first flight is decorated by two plaster caryatids. The plastered wooden supporting pier of the stairway is painted to resemble a trellis arbour hung with greenery. In the niche of the "arbour" is a plaster Cupid, a copy of the work of Étienne-Maurice Falconet (1716–1791). The second flight of each stairway makes a graceful turn round the arbour and continues to the second landing, semicircular this time, on which stands a table painted white, the colour of the stair. The last, straight flight mounts to the first floor, where the two stairways meet.

The Oval Hall

The central, most splendid and elegant room in the palace was built almost to the letter of Charles de Guerne's plan: only the doors were made lower and the ceiling painting was changed. Three French windows lead onto the semicircular porch of the park façade. Three rectangular, whitewashed oaken doors, with carved gilt fillets on each panel, lead into the Antechamber and the state apartments. The Oval Hall was redecorated after the 1820 fire. In the centre of the ceiling is a painting *Cupid and Psyche*, executed on canvas by Nicolas de Courteille. It covers the place where, before the fire, a skylight, or glazed lantern, illuminated the Oval Hall from above. Sixteen Corinthian columns of golden imitation marble are set in pairs round the walls. The facing of the columns and the stucco details of the capitals and entablature were done by the mason Savely Merkulov and by the stucco modeller Ivan Lazarev.

The three-tier chandelier made in Russia in the first quarter of the nineteenth century was installed in the 1830s. It was adorned with the figure of Nike, the goddess of victory. Apart from the chandelier there were two hundred lampions on the cornices of the gallery balustrades. The lower part of the hall was lit by floor candelabra over six feet high. Eight candelabra stood between the columns in front of mirrors hung on the piers. The armchair and the frames of the mirrors in the Oval Hall were made in the 1820s of poplar and Karelian birch. The upholstery of the chairs and the drapery above the doors leading to the park, golden silk with bouquets of roses, were possibly manufactured at Prince Yusupov's workshop in the village of Kupavna near Moscow. The oaken parquet panels, framed around the edge with water-seasoned oak, were laid in the 1820s by the carpenters Vasily Zhigaltsev and Nikolai Semionov. Two marble fireplaces with busts and candelabra on the mantelshelves were made at the same time by Giovanni and Carlo Silvestro Penno. The old fireside screens have been lost. The parquet, the pedestals and facing of the columns were restored in 1952.

The Imperial Room

A portrait gallery was a traditional feature of wealthy town and country houses in the eighteenth century. They often displayed portraits of members of the Tsar's family. The Imperial Room of the Arkhangelskoye palace shows portraits of the Russian emperors from Peter the Great to Alexander I, and hence its name. In the wall painting, done in 1820s, we see a prominent motif, typical of the late classicism, — fasces, ensigns of authority in ancient Rome. Since 1819 the central position in the room has been taken up by the large formal portrait of Alexander I by Jacques François Swebach and Henri François Riesener (1768–1828). The many portraits are framed by the garland painted round them on each wall. From the artistic point of view, the *Portrait of Princess Maria Fiodorovna*, a replica by the Swedish artist Alexander Roslin painted in the 1770s, and the *Portrait of Paul I* by Stepan Shchukin are of most interest. The bust of Peter the Great, a modified copy of the work of Carlo Bartolomeo Rastrelli (1675–1744), is by the eighteenth-century artist Carlo Albacini. The decoration of the room is completed by the mirrors over the chimney pieces and by the many sconces and girandoles of ormolu and crystal from the end of the eighteenth century. The appearance of the Imperial Room remains almost unchanged from the 1820s.

The State Bedroom

State bedrooms, in the eighteenth-century tradition, were usually very elegant. This room is the same size as the Imperial Room but its decoration is quite different from all the other apartments. Corinthian columns of white imitation marble on high pedestals mark off the alcove and boudoir. The columns were rebuilt after the fire of 1820 by Osip Ivanov and faced by Savely Merkulov. The moulded capitals are the work of Ivan Lazarev. The high corner stove of Dutch tiles was made in the 1820s.

It is said that the bed and other furniture in the early classical style belonged to the sister of the estate's owner Yevdokiya Yusupova, the Duchess of Courland, who died in the 1780s in Mitau (now Jelgava). The bedroom furniture was possibly brought from there. The cloth for the canopy, the draperies and the chair upholstery were made to old designs in 1963–65 by the Research Institute of Synthetic Textiles in Moscow. On the walls of the Bedroom are two paintings by Charles Amédée Philippe van Loo, which were cleaned in 1974.

The First Hubert Robert Room

This small octagonal room, painted in the 1820s, opens the west suite of the palace. Its main feature is the set of four paintings by Hubert Robert entitled *Ruins* (one canvas dates from 1779). Until 1837 the centre of the room was occupied by the sculpture *Cupid Bending the Club of Hercules*, a copy of the work of Edme Bouchardon (1698–1762). At the end of the 1830s it was replaced by the *Warrior Donning Armour* of Emil Wolff (1802–1879).

Of the early nineteenth-century furniture, only a painted wooden table with carved gilt stars remains. It was made by the serf craftsman Piotr Litvinov and gilded by two other serf craftsmen Semion Kotliarov and Semion Filippov. The mahogany furniture from the early nineteenth century was put here in the 1920s.

The Antique Gallery

The Antique Gallery occupies a central place in the west suite. Three glazed archways lead onto the side porch. The soft, silver-grey painting was done in the 1820s. The two tall rectangular tiled stoves were made by Ivan Basharin in the 1820s. The parquet, of the same period, was restored in the 1950s. Two basket chandeliers in various shades of bronze hung with prisms are from the late eighteenth century. In the early nineteenth century the room contained nine antique sculptures bought in the 1780s by Prince Nikolai Yusupov while he was the Russian envoy in Turin. Now Arkhangelskoye holds only four of these pieces, including the figure of a boy. The rest were taken to St Petersburg in 1837. Much of the painting and sculpture that was here in the first quarter of the nineteenth century is now lost: paintings by Jacques-Louis David and artists of his school hung there in the 1830s; *Minerva Protecting Fertility from Mars* by Abraham van Diepenbeeck was the centrepiece of this room (now it is displayed in the Study). There were also two portraits by Rembrandt (1606–1669), *Portrait of a Gentleman with a Tall Hat and Gloves* and *Portrait of a Lady with an Ostrich-feather Fan*. In 1834, they were taken to the Yusupovs' Petersburg palace; in 1917, they were transferred to their palace in the Crimea and, in 1919, taken abroad. Two years later they were bought by the American collector Weidener. Now they are housed in the National Gallery in Washington.

There remain in the Antique Gallery *A Cossack* and *A Turk* by Horace Vernet (1798–1863) and, a rarity in Soviet museums, companion paintings by Francisco Ramos-y-Albertos, *Heba* and *Ganymede*.

The Second Hubert Robert Room

This room ends the west suite of the palace. One of its glazed doors leads out to the side porch and the park, and the other, into the main courtyard, through the west colonnade of the palace. In 1816, the room was made octagonal by Strizhakov so as to match with the First Hubert Robert Room. The two Hubert Robert rooms contain identical chandeliers of carved and gilt wood, made in Russia in the first quarter of the nineteenth century.

The paintings of this room, in their subjects and colour range, are very different from grisailles in the Antique Gallery with their Empire symbolism. Bright, exotic birds form an ornamental frieze on the wall. The principal decoration of the room is the four large panels and the two small genre paintings — a rarity for this artist — by Hubert Robert. They have been there since the 1820s. The painting *The Pavilion of Apollo and an Obelisk* is dated 1801. In the lower left-hand corner the artist has depicted himself and his friend, the artist Jean Honoré Fragonard.

Until 1887 the *Cupid*, a statue by Mikhail Kozlovsky, occupied the centre of the room, emphasizing the axis of the west suite. It is now in the Hermitage in Leningrad. In the corresponding position at the other end of the suite was a copy of the *Cupid* by Edme Bouchardon.

The Tiepolo (Venetian) Room

This room, the largest in the north suite, was made out of two rooms by Strizhakov in 1816 to house the paintings of Giovanni Battista Tiepolo. They were hung on the walls opposite the windows. There were fireplaces on the side walls of the room but they were dismantled in the second half of the nineteenth century after the Tiepolo paintings had been taken to the Yusupovs' Petersburg palace. The room was then fitted out as a library and its walls lined with mahogany bookcases. In the 1880s and 1890s the insides of the doors, the mantelshelves and window seats were trimmed with mahogany. At the end of the 1920s the bookcases were removed and the Tiepolo paintings were returned to their former places. In the very first days of the War of 1941–45 these paintings, together with the other collections, were dispatched to the safety of the Urals. They were brought back after the war and hung opposite each other on the side walls of the room.

The well-known Soviet artist Alexander Korin restored the painting *Cleopatra's Feast* in 1941 and 1946. The other painting, *The Meeting of Antony and Cleopatra*, was restored in 1938–40 by Alexander Korin and Stepan Churakov. In 1965–68 this painting was thoroughly restored once more in the Grabar All-Russian Centre of Artistic and Scientific Restoration, Moscow.

There are other pictures which have been in this room since the beginning of the nineteenth century, including views of the outskirts of Rome by the German artist Jacob Philipp Hackert (1737–1807), commissioned by Prince Nikolai Yusupov. Around the walls are marble busts — copies of ancient originals — including *The Dying Giant* by Carlo Albacini, representing one of the images of the famous Pergamon altar. The other bust probably came from the studios of Santino Campioni, Paolo Triscorni and Carlo Silvestro Penno. Almost all these sculptures have been in this room since the first half of the nineteenth century. The statue *Venus Sleeping* by an unknown seventeenth-century French sculptor stood in various rooms in the first half of the nineteenth century before coming to rest in the Tiepolo Room. The mahogany furniture dates from the 1830s.

The Saloon (The Cupid Room)

The Saloon is situated to the left of the centre of the palace and placed symmetrically with the Imperial Room. The famous statue by Antonio Canova (1757–1822), *Cupid and Psyche*, was in this room until 1837, hence its other name. This statue is now housed in the Hermitage, Leningrad. As in the other rooms, the painting and parquet, the window frames and doors date from the 1820s.

An inventory of the 1830s mentions carved gilt furniture made in Russia in the 1780s and 1790s, and this furniture is still to be seen in the room. Its upholstery — golden brocatel — was made to the old pattern in the 1960s by the Research Institute of Synthetic Textiles, Moscow.

Since the 1830s the centrepiece of the room has been the painting *Andromache Protecting Astyanax* by Gabriel-François Doyen. The painting *The Death of Adonis* by Stefano Torelli has been there since the same time.

Among the paintings by French artists especially to be noted are *Apollo and Daphne*, a replica by François Le Moine, *The Startled Bather* by François Boucher, two seascapes by Claude Joseph Vernet, and the only canvas by Jean Tassaile in any Soviet museum, *Iphigenia Brought to Sacrifice*.

The Study

The last state apartment of the south suite, the Study, is the same size as the Saloon. Its walls are hung with the works of Dutch, Flemish, Italian and French painters of the seventeenth and eighteenth centuries. Most of the canvases were returned here between 1928 and 1931 from the former Yusupov palace in Leningrad. The original furniture is still here, made of poplar and Karelian birch at the beginning of the nineteenth century.

The Living Quarters (The Winter Rooms)

The living quarters are to be found on the east side of the palace and consist of three small rooms whose ceilings are only half the height of the state apartments. When the palace was built, a mezzanine was made between the first and ground floors. The ceiling of the winter rooms divides the doorways, leaving the lower, rectangular part as doors in the winter rooms while the fan-lights serve as windows in the mezzanine. From the outside this is almost undetectable and the east and west façades look the same. The walls of these rooms have no decorative paintings. A modest ornament, painted in the 1820s, borders the ceiling and only in the centre, where the lamp or chandelier hangs, is the ceiling decorated with a rosette or a star.

The Rotari Room
(The First Winter Room)

Until the beginning of the 1830s this room, adjacent to the Study, was the summer bedroom of Prince Nikolai Yusupov. The mahogany bed and armchairs which furnished the room in the first quarter of the last century are no longer here. In the 1830s, thirty-four studies of heads by Rotari, who spent his last years in Russia, were displayed in the room. They were probably acquired in the mid-eighteenth century by Boris Yusupov, father of Prince Nikolai Yusupov.

The Prince's Study
(The Third Winter Room)

The original early nineteenth-century furniture of this room has not been preserved. In the second half of the nineteenth century, it was fitted out with poplar and Karelian birch furniture made in the period between 1810 and 1820. The upholstery of the armchairs, similar in shape to those in the Oval Hall, golden silk with floral designs, was probably manufactured by serf craftsmen in Prince Yusupov's workshop in the village of Kupavna. The chief attraction in this room is the writing table of poplar trimmed with water-seasoned oak and gilt inlays. The slab between the table's legs is decorated with a gilt sphinx.

Among the family portraits in the room is one from the early 1760s of Prince Nikolai Yusupov as a child dressed in a guards uniform. Also worthy of attention is the bust of the Prince made around 1830 by Ivan Vitali (1794–1855). The French clock with the scene of Hector bidding farewell to Andromache and candelabra by Pierre-Philippe Tomire are excellent examples of artistic bronzework of the early nineteenth century.

At the beginning of the last century, a door led from the Third Winter Room into a "corner room" where a hoist was built in 1816 to carry meals up to the mezzanine and the first floor. The hoist was destroyed by fire in 1820. In the 1930s, the door was bricked up, and a new staircase constructed. The "corner room" became a stair well. The passage from the Third Winter Room to the Pantry, blocked up in the mid-nineteenth century, was reopened in 1977.

The Pantry was a low room with galleries above it. Food was brought here, through the "corner room", from the kitchen situated in the pavilion of the east wing. In the Pantry there was a serving hatch through which the food was passed to the State Dining-room.

The State Dining-room

After the fire of 1820 the State Dining-room was decorated with paintings in the Egyptian style, apparently by Nicolas de Courteille and Colombius. Among the bright stylized ornaments and figures are Masonic symbols — evidence of the interest in Freemasonry of Tiurin, the architect in charge of the restoration of the palace in the 1820s. In the 1910s these paintings were restored by Ignaty Nivinsky and in 1967, renovated by specialists from the Restoration Workshop of the USSR Ministry of Culture.

Of the original fittings in the State Dining-room four late eighteenth-century chandeliers remain, made of crystal and bronze of various shades, as well as a score of chairs with wicker seats from the late 1830s. *The Triumph of Claudius* by Gabriel-François Doyen hangs in its original place. Interesting items that made their appearance later are two late eighteenth-century oaken sideboards with large plaques of Wedgwood porcelain, which came in 1929 from the estate of Nikolskoye-Uriupino, also near Moscow.

The Library

Situated on the first floor, the Library consists of six rooms, whose doors, window-frames and pine parquet were the work of Semion Nikitin (1820s). The stoves faced with white Gzhel tiles with light-blue bands are the work of Ivan Basharin.

In the first quarter of the nineteenth century, this library contained twenty-four thousand volumes. One of the greatest of all the Moscow libraries, it took up not only the first floor of the palace, but also the first floor of the west pavilion. Many of the mahogany bookcases were made by local carpenters. In the 1830s, the whole library was moved to the west pavilion, but, in the 1930s, it was moved back again to the first floor of the palace. In the 1920s, about eight thousand books were given to the Lenin Library in Moscow. The Arkhangelskoye library retains, however, many unique volumes: books from Aldus Manutius' famous Venetian press of Renaissance times; Dutch books from the Elzeviers' printing house; books from the French Royal Press of the sixteenth century; first editions of Corneille, Racine, Rousseau, Voltaire, Montesquieu, Diderot, Calderon, Goldoni, Schiller, Stendhal and other eminent European literary figures. The library is remarkably wide-ranging: all branches of eighteenth-century knowledge are represented here. There is also a rich collection of Russian classics: editions of Lomonosov, Derzhavin, Zhukovsky, Pushkin and Krylov published in their lifetimes. The library contains many volumes of classical Latin and Greek authors as well as albums of engravings, atlases and journals from the time of the French Revolution.

Here also may be seen a life-size painted papier-mâché effigy of Jean Jacques Rousseau seated in a chair (a good example of French furniture of the late eighteenth century). The figure, chairs and a table were taken from an engraving after the painting by Jean Moreau the Younger (1741—1814), *The Last Minutes of Rousseau's Life*.

The Upper (Small) Terrace of the Park

The regular part of the park with its terraces and system of avenues and parterres was laid out at the end of the eighteenth century.

The terraces and the breast-walls decorated with balustrades were constructed to the design of Giacomo Trombara, — although his plan was largely altered during its execution. The Upper or Small Terrace (70 by 70 metres) with a parterre divided by a central path, joins the south façade of the palace. At the beginning of the last century it was adorned with symmetrically placed groups of marble sculptures: *Hercules and Anteus* and *Menelaus with the Body of Patroclus*. At the end of the 1820s the east and west sides of the terrace were planted with Siberian larch. In 1830, the groups of sculptures on the parterre were replaced by large marble vases. In the centre of the terrace a sculptural group was placed, on the main axis of the ensemble: *Hercules and Anteus*, an enlarged copy of the work by the seventeenth-century artist Stefano Maderno after a Michelangelo original. The marble vases on the balustrade of the Upper Terrace remain, as do the marble dogs and other sculptures, most of which were put there in 1810–12.

The Lower (Large) Terrace of the Park

The Lower Terrace with a fountain in the centre and two rectangular parterres is twice as long as the Upper Terrace (153 metres), but just over a third of its width at the centre (24 metres). The side parts of the Lower Terrace are large rectangles where the formal garden merges into landscape. At the beginning of the nineteenth century the fountain of the Lower Terrace was graced with the marble group *Cupid with a Swan* by an Italian artist of the late eighteenth century. On the parterres to the right and left of the centre of the terrace stood two large vases. In the 1830s and 1840s, four marble sculptures were brought here: *Artemis with a Deer, Apollo Belvedere* (both nineteenth-century copies of statues from the fourth century B.C.) and two identical statues of *Cupid Bending the Club of Hercules* (copies of Edme Bouchardon's original). In the late nineteenth century, *Cupid with a Swan* was replaced by *Cupids with Dolphins* (1889) by the Italian sculptor G. Giromello.

The balustrade of the Lower Terrace is decorated with forty-four marble busts and also has female figures and figures of lions, executed in the late eighteenth and early nineteenth centuries (probably by Italian artists working in Russia, such as Santino Campioni, Paolo Triscorni and Carlo Silvestro Penno). The collection of park sculptures, some two hundred items, is one of the largest in Russia. In 1810, there were more than fifty sculptures in the park, twenty-eight of them made of plaster. Most of the statues were brought here between 1810 and 1812. Many of them were badly damaged during the Napoleonic invasion in 1812 and were restored by Carlo Silvestro Penno.

The breast-walls of the Upper and Lower terraces were rebuilt in 1829 by Filipp Pavlov's team of masons under the supervision of the architect Vasily Dregalov. The niches of the lower breast-walls, which once contained busts, were bricked up, the stretches of wall between the rusticated posts were made smooth, and the white stone of the pedestals on which the pairs of busts had stood was replaced. At the same time the rectangular panels with bas-reliefs which had decorated the niches disappeared. The middle section of the wall was unaltered. The stairway has flights which go to the right and left and meet again at the top. Its sculptural decoration remains almost unchanged as does that of the Lower Terrace balustrade. Pairs of vases used to stand on the parapet of the stairway; they have been replaced by pairs of allegorical sculptures representing the four cardinal points. In 1822, there were a hundred and eight sculptures in the park. An eighteenth-century marble copy of the antique *Venus de' Medici* stands in the grotto in the centre of the supporting wall. The old, gilt bronze grille of the grotto in the form of sunrays has been lost.

The Large Parterre

The huge lawn (70 by 240 metres) is one of the most important components of the formal garden. In the first quarter of the nineteenth century lime-trees were planted along the paths on the east and west sides of the parterre, and kept at a height of five metres. The exits for the five short paths that cross the lawn are wide archways of greenery adorned with sculpture: there are ten statues on each side of the parterre. On its south side there still stand the marble figures of the so-called Borghese gladiators, early nineteenth-century copies of ancient originals. In the 1840s, old lime-trees were replaced by new ones pruned to spherical shape. Busts and statues were placed on the lawn facing away from the paths. The path along the southern edge of the Large Parterre divided it from the glasshouses and the flower beds around them. There was a fountain in the middle of the flower beds, but this part of the original layout was lost when new buildings replaced the glasshouses in 1933–37. Late eighteenth-century copies of ancient originals, the statues of Hercules and Flora, which once stood there were moved to a new place in the 1930s.

Memorial to Catherine

This pergola was built by Tiurin in 1819. Four of its columns were taken from the central entrance to the Caprice during its reconstruction in 1819. This structure has been restored more than once.

The Pink Fountain Pergola

This round pergola was built in the eastern part of the park in the nineteenth century, and it got its name from its columns of pink marble. The cupola is topped with a gilded bronze sphere. The ceiling and pendentive vaults were adorned with flower designs painted on canvas. The *Cupid with a Swan* group was brought here from the fountain of the Lower Terrace. The original designs were repainted in 1965 along the lines of surviving fragments.

The Library (The Tea House)

This building was constructed to Pettondi's design at the turn of the eighteenth and nineteenth centuries. Standing next to the Caprice, it was a pavilion with a rotunda in the centre flanked by two wings. The entrances to the wings were decorated with small porticos. The interior decor was done after 1810. In 1829, the wooden wings of the Library burned down, and the new façades of the surviving central part were made in 1834 by Dregalov. In the mid-nineteenth century the pavilion got the name of the Tea House. It was being restored from 1950 to the early 1960s. In 1936, the gravestone of Princess Tatyana Yusupova (1866–1888) was brought here. It had been made in 1902 by the Russian sculptor Mikhail Antokolsky (1843–1902).

The Small Palace (The Caprice)

Built at the end of the eighteenth century, the Caprice was originally a detached park pavilion. At first it was a single-storey building. A tetrastyle portico forming the main entrance was the focal point of its façade. In 1818–19, the first floor was built over the central part of the building. The new east and west façades were also decorated with tetrastyle porticos, the work was carried out by Naum Mitrofanov's team of masons to the design of Tiurin. In the single-storey wings two windows were converted into doors and the old portico at the main entrance was removed. Tiurin's plan was not completely realized. The decoration of the rooms in the Caprice had a palatial quality. Many paintings were hung here.

In the 1830s, this solitary palace was converted into ordinary living quarters. In front of the Caprice and the adjacent Library were thirty-five sculptures, as well as vases, busts and herms. Central place in the flower garden was commanded by *Cupid Bending the Club of Hercules*, a copy of an eighteenth-century original by the French sculptor Edme Bouchardon.

To the south of the Caprice an acacia pergola was constructed and decorated with eight statues which were removed to the Upper Terrace in the 1840s. At the same time all the sculpture from around the Caprice was transferred to the Upper Terrace. The iron fence with stone posts in front of the Caprice was probably dismantled in the early 1840s. In 1845, the decayed wooden columns were removed from the west façade of the Caprice. In the 1850s, the painting was erased from the façades, the forms of the doors and windows were changed and the paintings disappeared from the ceilings. The work was done under the supervision of the architect Koritsky and the serf architect Piotr Shestakov. In the 1890s, the wooden pillars of the east façade were replaced with brick ones. After 1914 the southern part of the Caprice was demolished and the palace was used as an outbuilding. Restoration of the façades of the Caprice and rebuilding of the demolished part was carried out in 1973–75 by the Restoration Workshop of the USSR Ministry of Culture.

The Holy Gates

The Holy Gates were built in 1824 to Tiurin's design. This archway, decorated with four Corinthian columns, is made of plaster-covered bricks. The columns and the socle are of white stone. The gates were so called because the road from the village main street to the church passed through them. The cross and the figures of angels decorating the gates have been lost.

The Stone Store Room by the Ravine

The Store Room is a two-storey building with an arched passage-way through the lower floor. A road went through this passage to a ford of the Moskva River. The building dates from the end of the eighteenth century. In 1816, a tower was built on it, which has not survived. In 1824, it was rebuilt by Beauvais.

The Yusupov Mausoleum (The Colonnade)

The architect Roman Klein (1858–1924) built this mausoleum in 1906–16 on the Yusup-

ovs' commission. The reason for the building of the family vault was the death of Nikolai F. Yusupov (1883–1908) in a duel. The mausoleum is a neoclassical, brick building, decorated to imitate granite facing, standing on a high, granite podium. In plan it forms a Greek cross. The central cubical block is surmounted with a domed rotunda. The moulded frieze of the rotunda was designed by Grigory Barkhin (1880–1968). The sculptural and moulded details of the façade were executed by Gladkov and Kozlov in 1912. Stretching towards the park, the colonnades, which join the central portico, command the area in front of the building to great effect. The original layout of these grounds by the architect Kelch has not been preserved. The modern layout (1960s) is by Victor Ass.

The interior of the Mausoleum has a striking wealth of decoration: the columns along the walls of the sanctuary have gilt capitals, as do the columns that are at the entrance to the hall. Moulded ornaments, paintings and gilt details adorn the vaults of the dome and the sanctuary, and the ceiling at the entrance. The interior painting was done under the supervision of Nivinsky, although the work was probably not completed. Restoration of the building took place in 1963–66.

The Picé Wall at the Church

The wall with its massive, brick archway was built near the north façade of the church to Tiurin's design in 1826. It is approximately 80 metres long. Between the brick posts the wall is made of clay inlaid with pebbles. At either end is a decorative, three-tier tower with a steeple. The first tier is of brick and the rest is wooden.

Church of the Archangel Michael

This brick church was built in the 1660s on the site of a wooden sixteenth-century church. It was probably designed by Pavel Potekhin, chief mason to the Cherkassky, and then the Odoyevsky, Princes. It is a small church with two chapels but with neither the normal parvis nor the usual crypt, and its decor is modest. An unusual feature is the placing of the chapels diagonally to the body of the church. The drums over the chapels are blind, but the drum of the main body is pierced with narrow windows.

The portals of the north chapel and the west parvis lead onto an open porch. The construction of the ceiling is interesting: the main vault puts the weight of the entire roof and of the drum of the central cupola onto the walls and two pillars near the west wall of the church. The church roof was originally made of planks, the cupolas being roofed with metal. The building was often altered, and the alterations of 1848 were particularly significant: the south chapel was widened, its cupola was moved to another position and the north-west porch was turned into an enclosed extention, as a result of which the church lost the originality of its former design. Immediately after the completion of the church it was floored with black and white ceramic tiles, which were replaced, in the late seventeenth century, with larger brick tiles laid in a herringbone pattern. In the 1900s, the floor was covered with bright flagstones. The eighteenth-century carved and gilt iconostasis has not survived. In the nineteenth century wooden galleries and wall paintings appeared.

The building was restored in 1964–68 by the Restoration Workshop of the USSR Ministry of Culture.

The Theatre

The theatre was built to Pietro Gonzaga's design, with the participation of Beauvais, in 1817–18. The interior decoration with a few adjustments followed Gonzaga's plan. The theatre's socle is made of brick and its walls are of wood covered with plaster. The brick came from the manège, demolished in 1817. The initial period of construction by the team of Osip Ivanov was supervised by Strizhakov; Tiurin also had a hand in the work, and Melnikov supervised work on the interior. The stuccowork on the capitals, cornices and other details was done by Timofeyev. In 1828, a new porch was built with two symmetrically arranged stairs decorated with marble vases which were evidently trans-

ferred from the Caprice. In 1857, Piotr Shestakov supervised restoration of the façades. The moulded frieze with bas-reliefs representing theatrical attributes was replaced by a whitewashed wooden one. The façades, walls and other wooden parts of the theatre were restored in 1940. The last major restoration took place in 1964–65 when the upholstery of the seats and the rails of the boxes were changed. The light-blue velvet, similar in shade to the original upholstery, was made by the Shcherbakov Silk Factory in Moscow.

Four incomplete stage-sets and a curtain remain from what Pietro Gonzaga designed for this theatre. In the 1920s they were thought to be lost, but in 1926 they were found in the basement of the theatre and put back on the stage. Nine watercolours by serf artists survive, depicting nine different Gonzaga's backdrops. The museum also contains several sketches drawn by Pietro Gonzaga himself. The entire stage-set of the Tavern survives (a backdrop, six side-scenes and a pelmet) as does that of the Malachite Hall (a backdrop, eight side-scenes and a pelmet). Of the Roman Temple only the backdrop remains, and the Prison is also incomplete. The average size of each backdrop is 6.5 by 9 metres. Fragments of the Dungeon set have also been preserved. Each stage set had a precisely determined position on the stage, and these different positions account for the variation in the dimensions of backdrops and side-scenes. These decorations have unfortunately deteriorated down the years. In 1941, they were removed to the Urals with the other collections. In 1945, they were brought back. They have been restored more than once (Restoration Workshops of the Moscow Art Theatre, 1946; Alexander Korin, 1949–50; Restoration Workshops of the USSR Ministry of Culture, 1963). As well as the decorations, the old stage machinery survives, a part of which was reconstructed at the workshops of the Bolshoi Theatre in Moscow.

АРХАНГЕЛЬСКОЕ
Дворянская усадьба XVIII–XIX веков

Альбом (на английском языке)

Издательство ,,Аврора''. Ленинград. 1984
Изд. № 1680. (8-10)
Printed and bound in the German Democratic Republic